2300600
5.99
LRCTEMPERL

101 FACTS ABOUT

GOLDFISH

Published by Ringpress Books Limited,
PO Box 8, Lydney, Gloucestershire,
GL15 4YN, United Kingdom.

Design: Sara Howell

First Published 2001
© 2001 RINGPRESS BOOKS LIMITED

ISBN 1 86054 226 3

Printed in Hong Kong through Printworks Int. Ltd.

0 9 8 7 6 5 4 3 2 1

101 FACTS ABOUT

GOLDFISH

Julia Barnes

Ringpress Books

1 Goldfish are beautiful to look at, and they are not difficult to keep. They are an ideal choice of fish if you are setting up an aquarium for the first time.

2 Keeping goldfish is not a new hobby. The Chinese first bred them 4,500 years ago.

3 The original goldfish was a dull brown colour, and looked very like a Crucian carp, which is the wild version of the species.

4 A gold colour was seen to occur in some fish, and these were taken away and became part of a special breeding programme.

5 In time, completely orange fish were produced, and the modern goldfish was born.

6 To understand your goldfish better, it helps if you understand how its body works and what the parts of the body are called (see below).

7 Goldfish, like all other types of fish are cold-blooded. This means they cannot keep themselves warm; their temperature depends on where they are living.

Inner ear

Eye

Nostril

Pectoral fin
(paired)

Pelvic fin
(paired)

Vent

Anal fin

Dorsal fin

Lateral line

Caudal fin

10 The goldfish's body is covered with bony scales that overlap each other. This helps the fish to swim more easily.

8 As fish live in water, they do not need lungs to breathe. They use gills which are very sensitive to the water around them.

11 The goldfish has a **lateral line** (pictured below), which is a fine line of sensors that runs along the side of the body. These pick up movement in the water.

9 The gills are found on the sides of the head, above the throat area. They are used to take in oxygen from the water, and to get rid of carbon dioxide from the goldfish's body.

The lateral line.

position in the water (pictured below) and do not move, often turning to a paler colour. They prefer to choose somewhere out of sight.

12 Goldfish have no eyelids and no iris (the coloured part in the human eye) so they cannot react quickly to changes in light. That is why goldfish usually dash for cover when lights come on.

13 Even though they cannot close their eyes, goldfish still go to sleep. They sink to a low

14 Goldfish can see colours and shapes, but not at any great distance. They can see in front and to the sides.

15 Although you cannot see a fish's ears, they can certainly hear. If the aquarium is knocked accidentally, you will see your goldfish dart away in fright.

16 A goldfish will usually live for around 25 years – but the **fancy** varieties may only live for about 14 years.

17 The oldest known goldfish was Fred who lived in West Sussex, UK. Fred lived to the grand old age of 41.

18 The traditional goldfish (pictured above) is a sturdy, no-nonsense fish with a colour that can be any shade from a strong golden red to a paler yellow gold. Some have patches of silver or gold on their bodies.

19 A wide range of different types of goldfish have been bred from the original goldfish, and these come in all shapes and sizes.

20 Goldfish are divided into two main groups: single-tailed varieties and twin-tailed varieties.

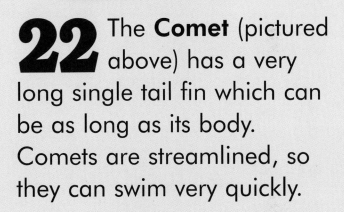

21 **Shubunkins** (pictured below) have a single tail fin, and are best known for their wonderful colours. They have a blue-silver body with shades of black, red, brown, yellow or violet.

22 The **Comet** (pictured above) has a very long single tail fin which can be as long as its body. Comets are streamlined, so they can swim very quickly.

23 Comets are usually plain yellow, but now you can also get Comets with a white body and bright red coloration along the back.

9

24 London Shubunkins (pictured above) have short fins and appear quite stocky in shape. Bristol Shubunkins (pictured below) have more developed, rounded fins.

25 Twin-tailed goldfish have a double tail fin, and they have a shorter body. They do not swim very well, and they can have health problems.

26 The **Fantail** (pictured below) has a short, round body and flowing fins. It swims pretty well, and is probably the easiest of the twin-tailed varieties to keep.

27 The **Veiltail** has a tail fin that hangs in folds, and the fin on its back (the dorsal fin), is very tall. These fish can easily damage themselves on rough, sharp or pointed objects.

28 The **Moor** (pictured above) is called a goldfish, but it is always black in colour. Their eyes stick out from the sides of their heads like mini telescopes.

29 The **Ryukin** has a shortened body, a steeply curved back, and flowing fins. When seen from behind, it resembles a butterfly. Despite is fancy appearance, the Ryukin is surprisingly hardy.

30 The **Lionhead** (pictured below) is a very poor swimmer as it has no back (dorsal) fin. It has an egg-shaped body, and a raspberry-like growth on its head.

31 The **Oranda** has a similar head but it does have a dorsal fin. The Red-capped Oranda has a white body and a red cap over its head. They are called 'gooseheads' in the United States.

32 There are many other weird and wonderful types of goldfish, such as the **Bubble eye** (pictured above), which has large bubbles which sit under its eyes, and the **Pompom** (pictured below), which has cheerleader-type pompoms on its nostrils.

33 These fancy goldfish are bred for their looks rather than for the fish's health and well-being, so they are probably best avoided. They are not a good choice if you are setting up your first fish tank.

34 Before you go to buy your goldfish, you will need to set up a suitable home for them. Tanks come in many different shapes and sizes, and are made of different materials.

36 It is better to choose an all-glass tank as plastic tanks tend to scratch more easily. The tank should have a lid fitted to it.

37 In a basic aquarium for goldfish, you do not need any extra equipment, beyond providing a gravel surface and some plants and rocks.

35 For the first-time fishkeeper, a basic rectangular tank is ideal. Buy the biggest tank you can afford – 2 ft long, 1 ft wide and 1 ft deep (60 cms x 30 cms x 30 cms) is fine, but a tank that measures 3 ft long, 15 ins wide and 15 ins deep (90 cms x 40 cms x 40 cms) is even better.

38 The problem is that, like all living creatures, fish need to get rid of waste products from their bodies. A process called **filtration** is used to break down the waste products so that they become harmless.

39 There are two basic types of filter. A **box filter** (pictured below right) can be suspended inside or outside the tank.

40 An **undergravel filter** (pictured above) fits across the base of the tank and is positioned under gravel.

41 Filters are powered by electricity so they have to be fitted and looked after by expert fish-keepers.

14

44 Excessive daylight will also encourage the growth of green **algae** on the glass sides of the tank.

42 Lighting will help you to see your goldfish more clearly. Lighting is usually fitted in the tank's **hood** which houses all the lighting gear and provides a lid for the tank. Expert help is needed to fit this equipment safely.

45 Your tank will be very heavy when it is full of water so you must make sure it is sitting on a sturdy table.

46 If you are using lighting or a filter, you will need to place the tank close to a power supply.

43 You need to decide where you are going to put your aquarium.

47 The next stage is the fun part of setting up an aquarium – deciding how it is going to look. The aim is to provide a healthy home which looks great!

48 To start with, you will need a backing sheet, which is attached to the back of the tank. These can be plain colours or they can be printed with exotic scenes of marine life – the choice is yours!

49 You will need to provide a gravel surface in the tank. You can buy brightly-coloured gravel, or you can go for a more natural look.

50 Goldfish like places to hide, and you provide these by using rocks and ornaments (pictured below).

you put it in the tank, and check with an expert fishkeeper to make sure it is suitable for a goldfish aquarium.

51 There are lots of different aquarium ornaments to choose from, ranging from deep-sea divers and shipwrecks to fantasy castles that create a magical kingdom. Let your imagination run riot!

53 Plants add colour and variety to a tank, and your goldfish will appreciate the contrast of swimming among the plants and swimming in open water.

52 Rocks and shells (pictured above) provide a more natural look. Make sure you wash everything thoroughly before

54 Check that the plants you buy are the right ones for a coldwater aquarium.

55 Among the plants that will do well in a coldwater aquarium are **Java Fern** (below left), **Sagittaria** (also known as arrowheads), and **Water Milfoil** (below right).

56 When you have bought the equipment, plus the plants, rocks, and ornaments, you can get the tank ready for your goldfish.

57 First, wash the gravel thoroughly before putting it in the tank.

58 The gravel should cover the bottom of the tank, with a gentle slope going from the back to the front of the tank. If you have an undergravel filter, this needs to go in before the gravel (pictured top right).

but you must leave it to stand for a couple of days to allow the **chlorine** that is present in water to clear before adding your goldfish.

59 If you have a box filter, this should be attached to the side of the tank.

60 Next, position the rocks and ornaments in the tank. Make sure these are washed first.

61 Now you can fill the tank with water. Ordinary tap water is fine,

64 At long last, you can go and buy your goldfish. Ask an experienced fishkeeper for advice on how many goldfish will live happily in your size of tank.

65 Fish get very stressed if they are overcrowded, and the water quality will also suffer, leading to ill health among the inhabitants of your tank.

62 It is better to fill your tank half-full, and then you can add your plants without getting your arms soaking wet!

63 If you have lighting equipment, this can be fitted before filling up the tank.

66 Go to a specialist aquarist store where experienced staff will be on hand to help you make your choice.

67 The fish you buy should show the following signs of good health (see below).

Scales: no sore areas or woolly fungal growths.

Body: well rounded – not excessively thin, but not too swollen either.

Eyes: bright and clear.

Movement: swimming effortlessly, though long-finned varieties will swim more slowly.

Fins: erect and undamaged.

Gills: rapid movement of the gills can be a sign of ill health, as is gulping at the surface of the water.

68 Do not try to mix the slower-swimming fancy types with singled-tailed goldfish. They don't get on well together.

69 Even if you have a big tank, it is better to start off with just a couple of goldfish. Add some more when you are confident that your aquarium is operating successfully.

70 The fish you choose will be caught in a net, and they will be put into a polythene bag of water to transport home.

71 When you get home, do not empty the fish straight into your aquarium.

72 Put the bag in your tank (pictured top right), and let it float there for at least 20 minutes. This allows the temperature of the water in the bag and in the tank to equalise, so your fish don't get a shock when they are released.

75 Goldfish food usually comes in flake form, and it will provide your goldfish with all the nutrients (food value) they need.

73 Do not be in a hurry to give your goldfish their first meal. It is better to give them a chance to get used to their new surroundings.

76 The biggest mistake made by most first-time fishkeepers is to overfeed their fish. If you feed too much, the food will rot in the water and will harm your fish.

74 There is a wide range of dried food for goldfish. The fish may come to the surface to feed or find the food at the bottom of the tank (pictured right).

23

79 If you want to give your goldfish a treat, buy some **daphnia** (water fleas) from your local aquarist store. Make sure you buy a small quantity so they all get eaten in one session.

77 Feed only as much as your fish will eat within 5-10 minutes. This amount should be fed twice a day.

80 Once you have set up your aquarium, it is pretty easy to keep it running. Carry out regular water changes to ensure that your tank stays clean and healthy.

78 A floating feeding ring will keep the food in one place so your fish will be able to find it easily.

81 In an unfiltered tank, 10-20 per cent of the water should be taken out twice a week. Use plastic tubing (pictured below left), about half an inch (12 mms) in diameter. In a filtered tank, this should be done every couple of weeks.

82 Dip the tubing in the water to fill it, and then place a finger over both ends. Put one end of the tube in the bottom of the tank and the other in a bucket which is below the level of the tank. As you release your fingers, the water will begin to flow.

83 Take the tubing from the tank as soon as you have removed enough water.

84 When you are filling your tank up with clean water, allow the water to stand for at least two hours before adding it to your aquarium to get rid of the chlorine that is present.

85 Algae, a fine green growth, is not harmful to the fish, but when it grows on the side of glass it spoils the look of your aquarium.

86 It can be removed quite easily with an algae scraper (pictured below), and this is a task that should be carried out every week.

87 Fish are not the easiest patients in the world, and so it is important to spot possible signs of trouble so you can seek the help of an experienced fishkeeper or a vet.

88 If you spend time watching your fish, you will be quick to notice if anything is wrong.

89 A fish that is showing signs of illness may be reluctant to feed. Its body may appear too thin or it may look swollen.

90 The fish may swim differently from normal, and may gasp at the surface of the water.

91 A fish that is suffering from stress may clamp its fins tight to its body.

92 Keep a close check for lumps or swellings on the skin, or for any injuries to the fins.

93 Fish can be treated successfully, but this is a job for those who have considerable experience handling fish, and preparing medication for them.

94 Goldfish are peace-loving creatures and will only become aggressive during the breeding season, which is usually in the spring when the days get longer.

97 For a successful hatching, the eggs have to be removed into a separate, pre-prepared **'hatchery' tank** – otherwise the adult fish will eat them.

95 It is only during the breeding season that you can tell males and females apart. A female's body (pictured above right) becomes swollen with eggs; the male (pictured above left) may develop white spots over the gills and on the front fins.

98 The eggs need to be kept at a temperature of around 70 degrees Fahrenheit (21 degrees Centigrade), and they hatch in around five days.

96 The female will lay her eggs, which are the size of tiny pinheads, on plants in the aquarium.

101 Breeding goldfish is a tricky business, and is best left to the experts. However, you will find that setting up an aquarium and caring for your goldfish is a great hobby, and in no time, you will become a proper fish expert!

99 The offspring, known as **fry**, look like tiny hairs attached to the plants.

100 At three days, the fry start swimming around the tank. They will need special fry food in order to develop into adults.

GLOSSARY

Algae: tiny, green plants.

Box filter: a filter that can be hung inside or outside the tank.

Bubble eye: a goldfish that has bubbles which sit under his eyes.

Chlorine: a chemical in tap water that is harmful to fish.

Comet: goldfish with one long tail fin.

Daphnia: water fleas which are fed to goldfish.

Fancy: ornamental types of goldfish.

Fantail: goldfish with a rounded body and flowing fins.

Filtration: a process that breaks down waste products in the water.

Fry: baby fish.

Hatchery tank: a tank for hatching eggs where no adults are allowed.

Hood: an aquarium lid that houses all the lighting gear.

Java Fern: aquarium plant.

Lateral line: a line of sensors on the fish's body.

Lionhead: goldfish with no dorsal fin.

Moor: black-coloured goldfish.

Oranda: goldfish with a raspberry-like growth on its head.

Pompom: goldfish that has 'pompoms' on its nostrils.

Ryukin: butterfly-shaped goldfish.

Sagittaria: aquarium plant.

Shubunkin: goldfish with a single tail fin and a silver-blue body.

Undergravel filter: a filter that lies on the bottom of the tank.

Veiltail: goldfish with a tail that hangs in folds.

Water Milfoil: aquarium plant.

MORE BOOKS TO READ

All About Your Goldfish
Bradley Viner
(Ringpress Books)

Look and Learn: Goldfish
M. Sweeney
(TFH Publications)

Pet Owner's Guide To The Goldfish
Steve Windsor
(Ringpress Books)

Taking Care of Your Goldfish
Helen Piers
(Barrons Juveniles)

WEBSITES

Goldfish information
www.geocities.com/Heartland/Hills/5086/care.htm

Goldfish mad
www.geocities.com/Tokyo/4468

Goldfish world
www.angelfire.com/wy/kokopalee/

Goldfish care
www.cyber-dyne.com/~Nunnie/goldfish.html

To find additional websites, use a reliable search engine to find one or more of the following key words: **goldfish**, **pet fish**, **aquarium**.

INDEX